Ventage STUFF

W9-DCB-308

$\mathcal{B}$ y the time we published **"Unplugged: The Vent III"** in 1997, just about all the readers and regular contributors to the AJC's extraordinarily popular column, **"The Vent,"** figured "best of" books were pretty much an annual thing. So did we.

We were all wrong. Sorry about that. We got busy.

And by the time we found a minute to pry open the Vent archives, nearly three years of your best work slapped us in the face, kind of like a wet pie in a Charlie Chaplin movie.

So, as we said in **Book One,** way back in the 1900s, here comes the Best of The Vent, anonymously contributed to blow off steam, to share your favorite gag line or just to offer a twisted bit of philosophy.

> May all your vents be heaven-sent.
> **– The Vent Guy**

Who's Responsible for This

Joey Ledford, the Vent Guy since 1994, puts on a mask and doubles as the AJC's Lane Ranger (told you we've been busy). He has compiled this collection, though hopefully not while driving.

Tom Bennett, veteran AJC editor and faithful follower of the Florida State Seminoles, made it happen. In the best Vent tradition, he grabbed the bull by the horns so we could ride this dead horse one more time.

Joey Ledford

Hyde Post, father of The Vent, cleared the way of all wags and scalawags, which is what bosses are supposed to do.

John Amoss, inVentor of the demonic Vent phone mascot, agreed to bring that puppy into the digital age, yet maintain that careful balance of decorum and mayhem.

Lisa Gardner and **Jim Smith** (not his real name) copy edited this book and although they strenuously objected to many objectionable items, they were summarily overruled every single time.

Inqui-Vent-ion

Don't you hate it when your afternoon drive-time radio talk show guy reads you the Internet humor you've already read when you should've been working that day?

I asked my friend how he managed to spend only $500 at the Gold Club. He said, "I got in free and didn't have anything to eat or drink."

If you can tell a lot about a person from his bathroom literature, how do you explain the three Vent books in my bathroom?

Is there a zoning law that requires each new strip mall to have a chiropractor's office, a tanning salon, a nail salon, a laundry and a Chinese restaurant?

Can the AJC reduce the size of the comics a little more? They're still too large for my microscope.

With Jane gone, who's going to keep Ted awake at the game?

After the commercial my son wanted to know
"What is reptile dysfunction?"
Thinking fast, I told him the man was having
trouble with his snake.

Is Wolfman's Donna married?
I'm looking for a wife who can sell furniture.

Why is it Amanda Davis is the one who always
gets to say Jerry Springer is up next?
Can't Russ say it sometimes?

I see that Martin Luther King Jr. has been nominated by the Catholic Church for martyrdom. Wonder how much they had to pay Coretta for that right?

If they know how many people didn't get counted in the last census, doesn't that mean they already knew the number of people?

I work on the 20th floor of my building and found out about a "secret" fire drill next week. If I take the elevator and leave the building early, am I guilty of premature evacuation?

The cell phone ad says "No Gimmicks!" at the
top, and "Certain restrictions apply"
at the bottom. I wonder which is true?

Who has more locations in Atlanta ?
the Waffle House or CVS?

Help me, fashion person! Do you think white
shoes will go good with my nipple rings?

Why do they call it a
one-night stand when
that's not what you do?

Man, if I hit the Lotto, do you know how many Big Game tickets that would buy?

Three dollars and 25 cents for a box of 20 Girl Scout cookies? What are they made of, gasoline?

How many men does it take to return a DVD? After watching it with my husband, I asked him to return it. He says he did – to the wrong store. Two weeks later, I found the DVD in the player.

Every time I see our governor, in my mind
I hear J.R. Ewing say,
"What's that idiot Barnes up to now?"

I identified two similar types of morons last week:
liberals who call Neal Boortz
and gays who call Dr. Laura.
They must get up in the morning and ask
themselves, "What can I do to be verbally
assaulted today in front of a live audience?"

Over the years you've printed five of my vents,
but I can only remember three of them. Can you
refresh my memory and reprint the other two?

Remember when the only Monica controversy
was about what Monica Kaufman
had done to her hair?

I wonder, will our children be playing president
instead of doctor from now on?

Is it me, or does that fire-ant guy on the radio do a more sincere apology than Bill Clinton?

Don't call and ask me, the telephone operator, if someone is available. How do I know if she's available? You expect me to leave this switchboard to find out? And besides, available for what?

I was watching Channel 2 news and the reporter said a woman broke two of her legs in an accident. Just how many legs did she have?

Why is it called Alcoholics Anonymous if you have to tell them your name?
Shouldn't it be called Alcoholics Unanimous?

Who was Absorbine Sr.?

So many of the candidates exclaim they're a "proven conservative." Who proves it?

TV reporters: Is there such a thing as a decomposed body that isn't "badly decomposed?"

Why do the people of Gwinnett County keep getting malls on top of malls when we here in Rockdale County have been waiting over a decade for just one?

Now that Saks Fifth Avenue is headquartered in Alabama, you think they will offer any decorator cement blocks to put the junk cars on in your yard?

Folks who live in the city may be urbane. Could folks who live a ways out be suburbane?

Are there any doctors out there who can surgically remove my mother from my back?

Does a still count as indoor plumbing?

How do I set my laser printer on stun?

Why do our kids have to take the Iowa Test of Basic Skills? Why can't we have a Georgia Test of Basic Skills with questions like, "Bubba's got three cars and he done traded for two more; how many cement blocks is Bubba gonna need?"

I asked my girlfriend,
"If everyone in this town was fingerprinted,
whose fingerprints would I find on you?"

The Psychic Friends Network is in Chapter 11
bankruptcy? Man, who saw that coming?

Is Captain Herb Emory a real captain
or is it kind of like Captain Kangaroo?

Upscale redneck or confused yuppie?
I saw someone take Starbucks coffee into the
Town Lake Waffle House.

Considering how fast the speed of light is, I wonder how fast lightning would be if it didn't zig-zag?

If a local TV news camera is covering a story and Bill Campbell is not there to stand in front of it, can it actually be considered news?

Let me get this straight: The FBI wants $37 million to catch Internet hackers when they can't even find a redneck in a cave on a mountain?

Why is it that the forecast on the Weather Channel never bears any resemblance to the one they do in the AJC. Are they consulting different psychics?

Why would NASA send a gizmo to Mars to gather rocks when we already have Rockmartians living west of Atlanta?

I finally saw "Air Force One," and I'm just wondering, could we swap the president we have now for Harrison Ford?

Rein-Vent-ing the Wheel

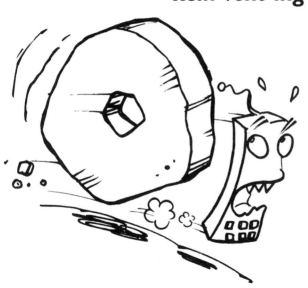

MARTA's crack writing team ("The approaching station is Medical Center") is now working for Delta. At the end of yesterday's flight, they wished me a great day "wherever your final destination may take you."

My daughter got a ticket for running a red light in Cobb. She said the yellow isn't as long there as it is in Gwinnett.

If you don't like your tea sweet, your okra fried and the word "y'all," Delta has 200 nonstops back to the North, y'all.

I was astonished to discover that the
Atlanta Toyota couple were cheating on us,
doing Orlando Toyota commercials.

That blonde in the hot little red car with the cell
phone stuck in her ear almost caused me to have
an accident on I-85 this morning when I tried to
catch up to her to see how cute she was.

Atlanta: where the streets are paved with
gold ... uh, I mean steel plates.

I guess my uncle is a redneck. A trooper stopped him on I-85 and asked, "Got some ID?" Uncle Tommy replied, " 'Bout whut?"

Carmageddon: The coming permanent gridlock on Atlanta's highways.

Rumor has it that Clark Howard owns the parking concession at the Birmingham airport.

The one good thing about gas prices being so high is it doesn't take me nearly as long to put in my $10 worth.

When the big overhead lighted sign on I-75 tells you it's "Less than 7 minutes to I-20," does it mean driving at the 55-mph speed limit or the more popular 80 mph?

My horoscope read, "You're going places and you can't be stopped." Apparently the cop who gave me a ticket hadn't read it.

There were more cars at South Cobb High
School this morning than at Cumberland Mall.
I counted them. I don't have much to do.

I heard on Channel 11 that a driver has a car
wreck every 14 seconds.
I'm sure he must be from Atlanta.

The electronic traffic signs on I-85 and I-75 are
not there to provide useful information, just to
make Atlanta look progressive.

I saw a company van rear-end a car today. The van had a sign, "How's my driving?"
I didn't have the heart to tell him.

Is it illegal for the six or seven police officers on the scene of an accident to actually direct traffic?

The cheapest place for gas in Atlanta:
Taco Bell. Get the bean burritos.

I must be spending too much time on the computer. Last night as I was crashing through the guardrail, careening down an embankment, I thought about hitting the "back" button.

You don't fully appreciate Delta's new aircraft paint scheme until you see it from a concourse window as the plane you were just bumped from takes off.

To the person who hit me from the rear on I-85 North Monday and took off:
You just ticked off the last Good Samaritan.

Forget all the self-help courses. Here's the five simple rules of life: Work hard. Save 20 percent of your earnings. Eat well. Exercise regularly. Hang up and drive.

I have never purchased a mattress. Anytime I need one, I just drive around I-285.

The trouble with bucket seats in an automobile is that not everyone has the same size bucket.

When I was a kid, all we had to do was just sit around and hope somebody would invent television so we could play Nintendo.

I've been watching Kroger's reserved parking spaces for pregnant women, and you'd be amazed at how many fat old men are expecting children.

I'm going to be a millionaire! I plan to sell hearing aids to Generation X-ers with $5,000 stereo systems in their cars.

Never get on an airplane
when you've heard someone
under the wing yell,
"OK, try it now."

Imagine those high school boys
on a weekend date, looking in her eyes
on a dark lonely road and saying,
"Come on, the president says it isn't having sex."

I just got a great new computer and I am gonna
brag about it for the next two weeks
until it is completely obsolete.

For those of you who've been out of town, the
approaching MARTA station hasn't arrived yet.

The problem with alternate routes is every time
you find a good one, some
doofus erects some speed humps.

I own a convertible and if anyone ever sees me
with my top down and my
windows up, please take my keys.

Sign seen on a tire store: "If your tires are as
slick as Clinton, you need new ones."

I was trying to figure out why almost all the
people who park in the fire lane at Kmart, Wal-
Mart and the grocery stores are fat
and suddenly it all made sense.

To the woman with the "What Would Jesus Do"
license plate: He wouldn't speed through my
neighborhood every afternoon
doing 65 mph in a 25-mph zone.

Yesterday, my eyeglass prescription ran out
and I promptly ran off the road.

Atlanta traffic engineers think that synchroniza-
tion has something to do with swimming.

To that car trying to barge into my lane: Get
thee behind me, Saturn.

I think it is wonderful that the city of Atlanta
decided to celebrate the release of "Titanic" on
video by placing slabs of the mighty ship's hull
over all the city's potholes.

It's amazing. I can drink coffee, shave, and talk on the cellular phone and still drive better than 90 percent of the people behind the wheel in Atlanta.

I've just discovered another use for those emergency flashers on your car. Apparently, if you turn them on, you can park anywhere you want.

If it were not for kudzu, just think how many junk cars, old hubcaps and abandoned outhouses we would have to look at.

I was pulled over by a trooper on 285. He said, "Ma'am you were weaving." "I wasn't weaving," I replied, "I was dodging potholes."

I lost a little more of my faith in the system when I saw a HERO truck getting towed down the road.

Now that Freaknik is over, is drunken driving illegal again?

It's getting to the point where a guy can't enjoy the simple things in life, like slicing a bagel and watching the butter melt on it without some idiot behind him honking his horn.

With all the new housing developments and the mud on their streets, we should change the license plate motto to, "Georgia on my car."

Delta: Don't Expect Luggage To Arrive.

There are much more embarrassing places to have pierced than your tongue, nose or ear. Those must be hard to explain at the airport.

My son is proof that anyone can be successful enough to drive a BMW or Mercedes. And besides, he looks so cute in his valet parking attendant uniform.

From a distance, too many taxis look like police cars. This is causing premature wear on my car's brakes.

The Course of Human E-Vents

You mean there really was black and white TV?
I thought that was just one my parents made up
to scare me.

Any child can tell you that the sole purpose of a
middle name is so he can tell when
he's really in trouble.

Elton John needs to do a song called
"Goodbye, Charlie Brown."

It's great the state Capitol has been restored to its 1889 look. Now the physical structure matches the mentality and ideas of its occupants.

I see where Fruit of the Loom is pursuing bankruptcy court protection. Will they be required to file some briefs?

I still prefer "Wheel of Fortune" to "Who Wants to be a Millionaire," and that's my final answer.

Now that Scooby Doo is employed at AOL, instead of, "You've got mail," you will hear, "Roo rot rail!"

The person who came up with the tongue ring is probably the great-great-great-grandchild of the idiot who conceived the necktie.

The other night my teenage daughter told me, "I don't know why I have to learn all this stuff in school. It's not like I'm ever going to be on a game show."

Some people worry about Nancy, others about Aunt Fritzi. I worry about Sluggo.

My son said, and I quote,
"My English teacher ain't gonna pass me."

When I voted, I felt like I was choosing the lesser of two weevils.

Being a Democrat in Gwinnett County is like being a deer in the NRA.

In 1999, the governor signs legislation outlawing bullying in our schools. Now it is 2000 and we discover that the biggest bully in our schools is the governor.

I took my first trip to the state Capitol today and learned a lot. A House representative gets up, makes a speech, says nothing, no one listens and everybody disagrees.

Seen on a bumper sticker in Buckhead: "Thank you for not shooting."

I went into an office at
City Hall and there was no one
there. I finally found a lady and
asked her,
"How many people work here?"
She said, "About half of us."

My theory is that Eric Rudolph became an FBI agent in '98 and has been hunting himself ever since.

I have just reread the U.S. Constitution and I couldn't find the part where it says my bathroom has to be counted every 10 years.

Please be accurate on the census forms, we need to know exactly how many people are being misrepresented by that Rebel state flag.

Another sign of the times: I asked my 5-year-old
granddaughter which she likes better, green
apples or red apples
and she said she needed to use a lifeline.

To the person who was disappointed with
Atlanta and plans to return to New York.
We're disappointed in you, too.
We invited y'all down for a friendly little war
and you set the place on fire.

A census worker came to my door and said,
"We're trying to find out how many people
there are in the U.S."
I told her, "Sorry, you've come to the wrong
house. I don't have the slightest idea."

Hey, Georgia Tech senior, don't be
so hard on the idiot freshman.
Eight years ago, you were one of them yourself.

I don't know much about drugs.
I thought uppers were dentures.

I tried using my age and treachery in a young singles' bar. I got beaten up and tossed out.

My 2-year-old is learning political doublespeak. The other day she said, "I not stinky; I poopy."

Vent Guy: I've told my students about the joys and satisfactions associated with venting, so prepare yourself to be gang-vented in the near future.

Today's frightful discovery: You can't see the TV
from a recliner while wearing bifocals.

I just looked around my cubicle and realized
I'm a Dilbert.

What's the difference between the Titanic and
the Atlanta Police Department?
The Titanic had a band.

The city is over budget, Atlanta police are as scarce as the spotted owl, sewers are collapsing, vagrants have overrun downtown and Buckhead, and all our delightful mayor wants to talk about is building a big fish tank. Brilliant.

With all the stories about rape, robbery, and murder in the paper, I almost missed the story about how the crime rate was dropping.

DiCaprio is actually Italian for "looks like a chick."

I'm glad we're finally getting rid of those
pesky trees so we can once again see
our beautiful billboards.

I was watching Mayor Campbell at his last press
conference and what worries me most is
he may be doing the very best he can.

A couple of more 1.5-million gallon sewage spills
by Atlanta and Alabama,
and Florida won't want that water.

It is so funny on the "Millionaire" show when someone phones a friend, or asks the audience and then says, "That's what I thought. I just wanted confirmation." Sure.

If you're going to vote for George W. Bush because you like his father,
consider this: Ralph David Abernathy Jr.

Note to Republican state legislators: If you want to get your speeding tickets fixed, you need to be in the majority party. This is still a democracy, you know.

We will miss Willie B. We're just sorry
he didn't live long enough to evolve
into a human being.

Don't feel sorry that Willie B. didn't
get a chance to evolve. As he was, he had
evolved further than most members
of the Georgia General Assembly.

Willie B. is dead and they say it was natural causes, but I'm suspicious. I'm calling for a full investigation of the pandas.

I loved Willie B. and I'm going to miss him, but he sure was a fat monkey.

Venture Capital

Separated at birth: Rep. Johnny Isakson and "The X-Files" Cigarette Smoking Man.

I'm trying to get out of debt. I might as well be trying to do away with Stone Mountain with a hand chisel.

What happens if a big asteroid hits Earth? Judging from realistic simulations involving a sledge hammer and a common laboratory frog, we can assume it will be pretty bad.

To those people who keep saying I am fat:
I am merely a victim of poor posture
and cheap tailoring.

My 22-year-old son thought the movie "The African Queen" was the biography of RuPaul.

Somebody gave my son the "Young Real Estate Developer kit" for Christmas and he has already cut down every tree in the neighborhood.

I don't like this at all.
My ATM bank statements still say, "We'll be ready when the year 2000 gets here."

I now know the true value of a dollar. I gave a panhandler one and he looked down his nose at me and didn't even say "thank you."

I just got Alabama's new state quarter.
It is two dimes and a nickel taped together.

I heard the new New York quarter is going to have a U-Haul on the back.

I see that an Ole Miss alumnus gave $100 million to combat illiteracy. It was really nice of him to help all those upperclassmen.

Poetic justice: Roberds, the king of "Buy Now, No Payments 'Til Next Year," has filed for bankruptcy.

When I'm finally holding all the cards, everyone decides to play checkers.

The way I'm interpreting a commercial I just saw, I can now get all the furniture I need from Rooms to Go and I don't have to pay for it until it's worn out.

Nothing says more about the state of education in Georgia than the number of people in the supermarket express lane who can't count past 10.

There was a Forest Service sign I drove by for years that said, "Trees Grow Jobs." This week, the trees and the little sign were plowed under for an entrance to a new subdivision. I guess the sign was right.

If they don't stop increasing the taxes on cigarettes, it's going to be cheaper to just buy pot.

I moved all the way to New Jersey and I still learn more about what is going on in Atlanta from The Vent than I can any other source.

Until "Who Wants to be a Millionaire"
offers to ante up enough money
to cover taxes, they should retitle the show,
"Who Wants to be a Six-Hundred
Thousandaire."

Reimbursing restaurants for removing
their cigarette vending machines
to make up for their lost revenue is like
paying the Mafia for not killing people.

Spending more time than I like waiting at the post office, I have figured out their secret. When the line gets to less than 12 people, they close a window.

We tried to form a neighborhood association because some of us wanted to restrict parking on the lawn to no more than two semi-tractors. But when it came to the really important stuff – like making slender blond wives mandatory – the women retaliated by trying to outlaw beer bellies, and everything fell apart.

Best thing to say if you're caught nodding off: "In Jesus' name, Amen."

I recently went to my 40th class reunion from nursery school. I didn't want to go because I had put on about 100 pounds since then.

My wife put so many cucumbers in my salad, it's become cucumbersome.

I'm tired of being called an aging baby boomer. For now on you can refer to me as a menopausal hippy.

I have the world's most perfect mother. Not only does she let me live at home for free, but she also tears out The Vent for me and leaves it on the TV tray.

There should be a new way to address the president: "Mr. President, you rascal you."

You know your husband has been out of work
too long when the little children in the neighborhood knock on the door and ask him
to come out and play.

It is true; you do catch more flies with honey
than with vinegar. But those strips you get from
the hardware store work best of all.

Monica, in regards to your closing salutation,
we really don't count on Channel 2 news.
We're using you for entertainment purposes only.

The devil lives
in vacuum cleaners
and all dogs know it.

You know you have finally arrived when the entire crew of the Waffle House calls you by your given name.

I just spent $700 to be told to take an aspirin a day. Do we have a great medical system in this country or what?

I saw this sign that said, "Come see how we fly." Don't they still use those big shiny airplanes?

Do AJC reporters have to go stand beside
buildings at night when they do
their stories like the TV reporters do?

So what do you think of Atlanta's new
17-digit dialing system?
That's where you dial seven digits, go
"Darn it," hang up and dial 10 more.

Hey, Delta, why don't I get frequent flier miles
for circling Hartsfield?

We have a billion-dollar airport with restrooms
that would embarrass Bulgaria.

When I see smokers toss their butts
out of their car window, I find myself
wishing I could toss their butts into the road.

I was driving down the road in Duluth and I
saw a street called Four Wheel Drive.
Are we in Georgia or what?

The reason the University of Georgia fell from No. 1 to No. 4 on the Princeton Review's party school list is because my roommate and I graduated.

If the FBI really wanted to catch Eric Rudolph, they would send a busload of Gwinnett County developers into those mountains and it wouldn't be long before he'd have no place to hide.

Obesity has now been linked to religion and to the number of hours you watch TV. And all this time I thought it had something to do with food.

Public TV says, "If you want a copy of this program, send $49.99." If I wanted a copy I could just press RECORD on my VCR.

The little tag says my new $70 shirt was inspected by Pauline. It has a tear on the sleeve. Way to go, Pauline.

I asked a complete stranger who had spoken to me at the Governor's Ball how he knew I was a UGA graduate. He said, "I noticed your ring when you were picking your nose."

I know our economy must be going great in creating new jobs because I have gotten three of them.

My theft losses weren't high enough to claim on my 1999 tax return. I hope they steal more this year.

Hey, I'm a Southern Baptist and trust me,
our religion is not organized.

At the end of the day when the stock market
closes and it loses 207 points, why does all the
staff there on Wall Street stand up and clap?

Attention DOT sign makers and the people who
do the graphics for school closings on TV:
DeKalb is ALWAYS spelled with a capital "K."

When one of those long-distance phone company salesmen starts his spiel, just tell him, "I don't have a phone," and hang up.

If you don't think we live in a complicated world, try reading an insurance policy.

For a state that ranks so low in education, Georgia sure bans a lot of books.

I think Taco Bell should tell you they're going to give you only two packs of sauce before they take your money.

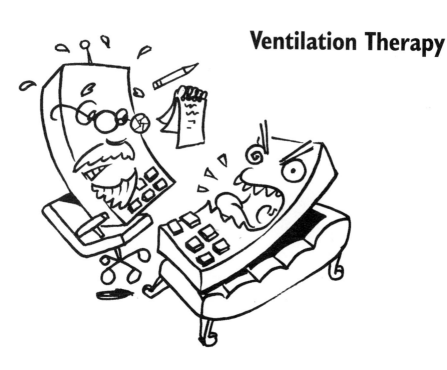

I love my dog like a member of the family, but if he ever fell unconscious on the floor, I just don't think I could perform mouth to mouth resuscitation on him.

If you combine hip-hop with country and western, you get a song about a man, his dog, and the hood.

I recently visited Graceland and I left with one enduring thought: Elvis is buried in the back-yard like a darn hamster.

I'm coming from Cumming
to Morrow tomorrow.

I knew this Y2K thing would be a bust.
In fact, I'm writing President McKinley
tomorrow to complain.

The last house the Clintons owned
was a little bungalow in the 1970s, so it's hard
to believe Hillary has two moving vans
full of stuff to put in her new house.
Somebody better inventory the White House.

To the lady in the express line in the
Fort Gillem commissary: a limit of 15 items by
cash doesn't mean 23 items by check.
And you're not forgiven because
you had a nice butt.

Progress among Georgia legislators:
Old millennium-lap dances;
new millennium-laptops.

I didn't even get to brush my teeth today;
no electricity.

My neighbor has started
a small garden near the street.
He says he plans to grow corn on the curb.

With Kathie Lee quitting the talk show,
maybe Regis will too.
I've been worried about him working too hard.

If someone calls me fat, I don't get angry.
I just turn the other chin.

I just read that Prozac is no longer
the number one selling anti-depressant drug.
That makes me feel sad.

A reason to smile: Every seven minutes,
someone in an aerobics class
pulls a hamstring.

It really ticks me off when I order
the Biggie fries and it's only half-full.

My dog treats me like family.
The cats treat me like staff.

'Tis better to have vented and not been printed
than to have never vented at all.

I took one of those drugs for nervousness.
Now I have headaches, nausea,
high-blood pressure and can't see.
But at least I'm not nervous anymore.

The world does not beat its way to your door
until you are in the bathroom.

You can tell it's going to be
one of those days when the first thing
you think when you get up is that
you're going to take a nap when you get home.

Seen on a church sign: "If you are waiting on a
sign from God, this is it!"

If you took all the people who fall
asleep in afternoon meetings
and laid them end to end,
you'd be a lot more comfortable.

Somebody said it's frightening
how much topsoil we're losing each year,
but I told that story around a
campfire recently and nobody got scared.

Ecologists tell us we shouldn't
hunt any animal to extinction,
but the squirrel should be an exception.

Wah hayell, I didn't know until today
that the 2004 Olympics are going to
be in Athens. How 'bout them Dawgs!

If you're going fishing with a Baptist,
bring another Baptist with you.
Otherwise, he'll drink all your beer.

I think my vents would sound so much better
if I could use curse words.

Reading The Vent makes you feel like
the Navaho who looked across the desert
and saw the mushroom cloud from the first
atomic blast. He was sending smoke signals
and he thought, "I wish I'd said that."

Minor fame is when your vent gets printed.
Major fame is when a bunch of people
call in vents arguing with your vent.
But true immortality is when
someone writes a letter to the editor
complaining about your vent.

They say Starr's investigation
cost each of us 15 cents.
I've gotten my money's worth just in dirty jokes.

The White House lawyers are depressing me,
because now I'm not even sure
if I've ever had sex.

The downside of being printed in The Vent
once or twice is that subsequent rejection
seems so personal.

President Clinton needs to come clean and
Monica Lewinsky needs to dry clean.

Save the whales. Collect the whole set.

Don't let the light of your life
come from the bulb in your refrigerator.

Some people have a way with words.
Some people . . . ugh . . . not have way.

Debris: De cheese you eat on de cracker.

I always look for jobs that have drug testing
because I studied.

I quit smoking cold turkey.
It was too hard cramming it into my pipe.

Looking back over the last 45 years,
I realize my life would be so empty
if I hadn't seen all that TV.

Be careful with those new relaxed-fit jeans.
I wore mine and almost fell asleep at the wheel.

There seems to be great confusion among
Atlanta drivers as to exactly how many
are supposed to go through on a red light.

My wife is allergic to peanuts.
When she's exposed to them,
her face blows up and she needs medication.

The more Civil War re-enactors I see,
it's clearer to me why we lost the war.

Would you please ask Sen. Trent Lott
and the Christian Coalition to please
send me a copy of the Gay Agenda?
I'm gay and have never received my copy.

Hey, I know that aliens exist
because I saw their offspring
walking around Little Five Points yesterday.

It's really nice having a young kid.
I hold him in front of me when I go out to get
the paper in the morning and
I don't get any spider webs on me.

"Lawmakers" sounds like something from the
Wild West: "Better git outta town quick Billy,
the lawmakers are a-comin'."

Be nice to other people.
They outnumber you 5.5 billion to one.

This is not the mortuary.
Please stop misdialing and asking me
if we are holding Aunt Kate's body.

I called the paper to put in an ad,
but I couldn't tell the lady about it
because it was classified.

Twenty-four hours in a day; 24 beers in a case. Coincidence?

I have to exercise early in the morning before my brain figures out what I am doing.

The Oxygen Channel is absolutely choking the breath out of me.

Some of the vents lately sound like they came from the Vent Outlet Store in Boaz.

It'll never replace red-eye gravy, but my ostentatious Yankee friend showed me that grits taste pretty good with hollandaise sauce.

I hear that when they finish the flooded town
water ride at Stone Mountain Park
you'll be able to choose between
the Smallpox Outbreak Funhouse and the
Lynch-A-Horse-Thief Hayride.

Ventricals
(And Other Heartbreakers)

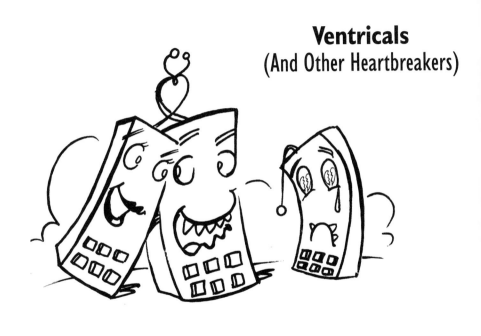

I asked my new girlfriend if she smoked after sex.
"I don't know," she replied.
"I've never looked."

Is it proper for my female doctor to
ask me at a crowded New Year's Eve party
how my Viagra is working?

North Georgia farmer looking for wife
who can clean, cook and sew.
Must own a tractor.
Please send picture of the tractor.

Women will never be equal to men until they can walk down the street with a bald head and a beer gut and still think they are beautiful.

I read in the paper about some guy wanted for a sexual battery charge. That sounds promising. I need mine charged, too.

Women close their eyes when they kiss because they can't stand to see a man have a good time.

With my history of attracting
the wrong kind of men I am surprised that
Eric Robert Rudolph hasn't found me by now.

To my male roommate: That humming sound that
you hear coming from the bathroom is my electric
toothbrush, so quit listening at the door.

They say old age brings great character and
wisdom. Frankly, I'd rather have cute buns.

I always introduce my girlfriend as
my potential future ex-wife.

My girlfriend told me she wanted to get married
and I told her I didn't want her to.

If Viagra commercials are to be believed,
all you get is a man who dances.
Maybe that's improvement enough.

When I gave blood, they asked me if
I had paid anyone for sex in the last
six months. I said, "No, but do you think
that would work with my husband?"

When I gave blood and they asked me if I had
paid for sex in the last six months, I replied,
"Does dinner and a movie count?"

My new girlfriend says sex gets rid of her
headaches. What a deal!

My wife left me for my son's soccer coach.
Do I still need to pay the soccer fees
for this year?

My girlfriend is such an optimist that minutes
after the tree crashed through her
dining room roof, she said she liked
the nice, fresh pine scent.

A man will pay $200 for a $100 item that he needs.
A woman will pay $100
for a $200 item that she doesn't need.

Ever since my fiance got his master's degree in
astronomy, he calls himself the master of the universe.

I'm leaving my husband for the copier at work. I
see it more than I see him and it puts out more.

What's wrong with women these days?
My wife went out and bought a piano after
Christmas and said that was my present to her.
And I'd already given her a $12 meat themometer.

During a conversation with a friend today,
he said he was lucky because he was married
to an angel. I told him he was very lucky because
my wife is still alive.

All I ask for is a guy who will treat me
as good as I treat my dog: Play with me every
day, let me sleep with you, buy me new toys,
and spoil me rotten.

This menopause thing is tearing my life apart. I
think my wife is also having a rough time with it.

One of the benefits of being a woman: If we
marry someone 20 years younger than us,
we're aware that we look like an idiot.

One of the benefits of being a man is if we marry someone 20 years younger than us we're too happy to care if we look like an idiot.

The ultimate hypocrisy: Larry King, married eight times, questioning Darva Conger about how SHE made a mockery of marriage.

I met a beautiful girl at a bar and
I asked her, "What is your sign?"
She replied, "No trespassing."

When I asked a girl in a bar, "What is your
sign?" she said,
"Slippery when wet."

My wild oats have turned
into prunes and All Bran.

The manager of the oil change place asked for my business card, saying he has a single friend. I must have "desperate" stamped on my forehead.

To the guy who fell off the treadmill at the health club trying to check me out: Thanks! That was the best compliment I have ever received.

I asked my wife what I could do to get her
interested in sex and she said,
"Leave town."

My ex-wife has accused me of being with five
different women and I can swear on the Bible
that I've only been with three
and those three weren't on her list.

I asked my wife, if I died and she remarried, would she let him drive my pickup truck?
"That crummy thing?" she replied. "Heck no. He has a new one."

I don't care who's elected president, but I sure hope their wife will wear dresses because I am tired of seeing Hillary in all those pantsuits.

My wife has her own version of money laundering. She cleans out my pockets every night while I am asleep.

You know you're a dirty old man when the sweet young thing in the bikini that you've been flirting with at the pool had to get out during adult swim.

A man and his wife went to bed one night and the man was getting very frisky and asked his wife if she was in the mood. She answered, "Not tonight, dear. I have a headache."

The man said, "Is that your final answer?"

She said yes and the man, replied,

"OK, then I'd like to phone a friend."

As I pulled into a parking lot, two young men were
really giving me the eye. I walked past, smugly
thinking "Yes! I've still got it."
Then one called out, "Ma'am,
do you want to sell that Isuzu?"

Definition of an optimist: a woman who loads up
the CD changer before making love.

A Vent for All Seasons

Wish I wasn't living in the land of pollen/ My nose itches, and my eyes are swollen/ Sneeze away! Sneeze away! Sneeze away, Dixieland!

Don't you love the changing of the seasons from pollen to smog?

I think weather commentators should be required to take a course on the actual sizes of baseballs and golf balls for proper hail size assessment.

I sure am getting tired of listening to those songs from the 1900s on the radio.

I have five children, have lived in numerous Northern cities and never recall schools announcing closings just in case the weather does what the meteorologists predict.
No wonder Northerners think we Southerners are not too bright.

Wow, it's spring! Time to open the windows and blast your neighbors with your stereo.

It sounded like my husband was watching a TV show depicting a passionate sex scene. When I went to investigate, it turned out to be two old men standing in a boat reeling in a fish.

To all our friends and neighbors we haven't seen all winter: Our pool will be opening in two weeks. We know we'll hear from you soon.

To the person who stole my gold cross and silver angel at my garage sale: thanks a lot. That was real Christian of you.

My grandfather had a farm. My father had a garden. I have a can opener.

John Wayne was always hip. Last night, I was watching the Duke in a 1945 war movie and he turned to another actor and said, "What's up?"

Pollen, pollen everywhere and
oh, those trees do stink.

Remember the next time someone wants
to take you under their wing that it's
really just their big old smelly armpit.

I wish John Denver were here so he could sing,
"You fill out my census . .."

I've heard that the rings
of Saturn are composed entirely
of luggage lost by the airlines.

When you're older, only two opinions count: Your children, because they can put you in a home and your neighbors, because they can call your children.

I may be a little sick, but when I see those people on TV who won't evacuate and say they want to ride out the hurricane, I start rooting for the hurricane.

When the garage sale ad says,
"Great for college students," it means it's junk
you wouldn't put in your house.

The Vent Guy is like Santa Claus.
You can't see him, but you enjoy the
evidence of his existence.

You know you are having a bad day when you
catch your kids looking through your closet for
something to wear to Nerd Day at summer camp.

With this being the warmest year in the record-
ed history of planet Earth, I believe that Global
Warming is real, and I theorize that it is being
caused by extraordinary numbers of Baby
Boomer women now experiencing Hot Flashes.

Southerners don't have snow accidents because
of black ice or the lack of snow tires.
We crash while looking back into the truckbed
to see if the dog has frozen.

It was weird watching the presidential
anti-apology. I kept thinking any second,
he was going to say,
"Live from New York, it's Saturday Night!"

Rhett, you'd better hide Scarlett in the closet.
Bill Clinton's coming to Atlanta today.

It should be obvious to Chelsea why her mother
never let her have a White House slumber party.

Now I'm beginning to suspect President Clinton
inhaled after all.

You can say whatever you want about someone as
long as you include the phrase,
"Bless his heart."

If they really want to get rid of kudzu they
don't need a new bug. Just give it a Latin name,
designate it a garden flower, sell it at Pike's,
and let my wife try to grow it.
It's worked for everything else in our yard.

The government could save a lot of money
if it would dump the surgeon general and go
with a chiropractic colonel.

From now on, the seal of Gwinnett County
ought to include a picture of a
bulldozer knocking down a tree.

We don't need a war on drugs in Atlanta.
We need a war on drugstores.
Please stop building them. We have enough.

To the lady on the toothpaste commercial who's complaining that her dentist father checks her teeth every time she gets in the car: You oughta be glad he's not a gynecologist.

I love to see a news story Only on Two and then switch channels and see it again First on Five.

There's a sign in front of a building that says:
"Midtown Urology Dentist."
Sorry, but I'm not going there.

I went to the barber about 10 years ago and had
a little cut off the top and it never grew back.

I sure hope they don't pass that bill that would
prevent food stamps from being sent to the
dead. My late Uncle Henry needs those.

My rural county tried a school uniform program but had to drop it. With all that camouflage clothing, we kept losing the kids at recess.

If my call was really important to you, you would have more customer service people so I wouldn't have to spend 20 minutes on hold.

A bus station is where a bus stops.
A train station is where a train stops.
My desk is a work station.

My neighborhood is so tough that
every time you close a window,
you smash someone else's hands.

Major League Vent

When choosing the top four greatest athletes of the century, how can ESPN include three-time World Champion Muhammed Ali and six-time World Champion Michael Jordan, and not include 14-time World Champion Ric Flair?

If the NFL really wanted to "punish" Atlanta for not selling out the Falcons' home games, they'd nix the blackout and show them on TV twice.

Had Chris Rock said the same things on stage that John Rocker said to Sports Illustrated, the audience would have laughed.

Had Chris Rock said the same thing on stage that John Rocker said, he would have been joking.

Elect me dictator and I promise to do away with the designated hitter, night baseball on the West Coast and $5 soft drinks.

I see that Michael Jordan has been named president of the Washington Wizards. Now we have two presidents in Washington who know how to score.

Northerners who stand in front of the "Today" show window carry signs that say "Hi Mom" and "Hi Peoria," but Southerners seem to always have signs saying things like "Go Dogs" or "Roll Tide."

Every time I look at the sports section, the first picture I see is somebody with their arms over their head showing a lot of underarm hair. That is sickening. They should shave if they are going to do that.

Why is it my husband can't remember to take out the garbage but can remember every single detail of every shot he hit for 18 holes?

To the man who thinks basketball is an incredibly boring and dull sport: I think I love you.

I gave up jogging for my health when my thighs kept rubbing together and setting my pantyhose on fire.

If Rocker gets released
by the Braves, he can always get
himself a job as a
conservative talk show host.

After watching the Tech and UGA faithful beat up each other about the quality of the sewers under their stadiums, I think I am now beginning to understand the true depth of the rivalry.

The only reason I would take up jogging would be so I can hear heavy breathing again.

Remember the good old days when basketball uniforms fit and palming the ball and traveling were violations?

OK, people, the "air ball" chant used to be fresh, but now it's as annoying as the wave.

What do you call 200 white guys chasing one black guy? The PGA Tour.

So, if John Rocker is traded to Montreal, do we call him Jean Roque?

It's time to rename the Atlanta Thrashers
the Thrashees.

WSB reported that the game in Japan was "the
first Major League Baseball game played outside
the United States." It makes you wonder what
state Toronto and Montreal are in.

OK, Braves, I give up.
What channel are you on?

The Vent Guy has shut me out so many times he must think he's Greg Maddux.

If criminals received justice as quickly and decisively as overtime in college football, this would be a much better country.

I watched a good bit of the X-Games and I didn't see Mulder or Scully once.

Who says women have to exercise to have beautiful legs? I've gotten mine from wearing high-heeled shoes for years, and I'd put them against any athlete's. (Did that come out right?)

There were so many swooshes on the college football uniforms this week that NCAA must now stand for the Nike Collegiate Athletic Association.

So UGA dropped to No. 4 on the party school list. That wouldn't happen if they would redshirt their partiers!

A local golf discount store burned to the ground. There were too many irons in the fire.

My wife started wearing jockey shorts. Now she spits all the time and wants to watch Monday Night Football.

If Georgia Perimeter College had a football
team, the average weight of its
offensive line would have to be 285.

I said Chipper Jones looks like someone poured
into his uniform and my wife
said she'd like to pour him out of it.

Evander Holyfield: knocking men out
and knocking women up.

Actually, Steve DeBerg wasn't the Falcons'
first choice for a back-up quarterback,
but unfortunately, Sid Luckman died.

Watching the Peachtree Road Race I
observed that at the end, as the crowd
gets thinner, the crowd gets fatter.

My girlfriend sat between two big people at the Ted last weekend. Thank goodness she's skinny. When the big people stood up, so did she, and her feet never touched the ground.

I have not been to a Braves game at the Ted. How do I get there off the Hank?

I love it when baseball players fight. I really enjoy watching rich people hurt each other.

Greg Maddux has got to be the luckiest pitcher
on the face of the Earth.
Every time he pitches, the other team only
scores one or two runs.

I'm tired of hearing "your Atlanta Braves" and
"your Atlanta Hawks," all the time.
They aren't mine, they're Ted's.
If they were mine, I'd have free owner's box
seats and complimentary brewskis.

I am offended people insinuate Georgia football players take easy classes when everyone knows Tech players' class of choice is "Hydraulic Principles of the Keg."

Apparently someone forgot to tell Ray Lewis that the official getaway car of the NFL is the white Ford Bronco.

My high school football coach was tough, but he was willing to compromise. He told us no facial hair, but you can keep your eyebrows.